I0820952

DINOSAURS

APATOSAURUS

BY ANGELA LIM

An Imprint of Abdo Publishing
abdobooks.com

abdobooks.com

Published by Abdo Publishing, a division of ABDO, PO Box 398166, Minneapolis, Minnesota 55439.

Printed in the United States of America, North Mankato, Minnesota.
052025
092025

Cover Photo: Daniel Eskridge/Shutterstock Images
Interior Photos: Kurt Miller/Stocktrek Images/Science Source, 4–5; Shutterstock Images, 6, 9, 20–21; Millard H. Sharp/Science Source, 8, 15; Red Line Editorial, 10; Phil Wilson/Stocktrek Images/Science Source, 12–13; Nicholas Courtney/Shutterstock Images, 16; James Kuether/Science Source, 18–19; Used by permission, Uintah County Library Regional History Center, all rights reserved, 22; Elena Duvernay/Stocktrek Images/Science Source, 25; Universal/Allstar Picture Library Limited/Alamy, 26; Sebastian Kaulitzki/Science Source, 28–29

Editor: Kari Cornell
Series Designer: Mary Shaw

Library of Congress Control Number: 2024949187

Publisher's Cataloging-in-Publication Data

Names: Lim, Angela, author.
Title: Apatosaurus / by Angela Lim
Description: Minneapolis, Minnesota: Abdo Publishing, 2026 | Series: Dinosaurs | Includes online resources and index.
Identifiers: ISBN 9781098297329 (lib. bdg.) | ISBN 9798384919841 (ebook)
Subjects: LCSH: Apatosaurus--Juvenile literature. | Dinosaurs--Juvenile literature. | Herbivores--Juvenile literature. | Paleontology--Juvenile literature. | Extinct animals--Juvenile literature.
Classification: DDC 568.19--dc23

CONTENTS

Apatosaurus often traveled in herds for protection.

CHAPTER 1

GIANT GRAZERS

Near a forest, *Apatosaurus* (uh-PAT-uh-SOHR-uhs) gather. The dinosaurs crush the grass with their huge feet. They hear a sound and turn their heads. A much smaller dinosaur quickly scrambles away. The giant *Apatosaurus* is too big to hunt.

Apatosaurus was 75 feet (23 m) long. Its long neck helped it reach vegetation in shallow water.

The small dinosaur will need to search elsewhere for a meal.

The largest *Apatosaurus* in the herd lets out a bellow. It stretches out its long neck. It grazes hungrily on low-lying plants. Others in the herd follow its lead. These dinosaurs need a huge amount of food to survive. They eat up to 880 pounds (400 kg) of plant material each day. This is equal to the weight of a large motorcycle.

Suddenly, another large dinosaur crashes through the forest. It is an *Allosaurus*. The **predator** reveals its sharp teeth as it roars.

The *Apatosaurus* huddle together for safety. The *Allosaurus* lunges. But the large *Apatosaurus* whips its long tail before the other dinosaur can get too close. The movement causes a loud boom to ring through the air. The noise startles the *Allosaurus*. It quickly runs away. The *Apatosaurus* herd continues grazing in peace.

Apatosaurus skulls and bones have been discovered in Wyoming, Colorado, and Montana.

What Are Dinosaurs?

Dinosaurs are a group of ancient reptiles. They lived during the Mesozoic Era. This era began more than 250 million years ago.

Within the Mesozoic

The Mesozoic Era can be divided into three periods. They are the Triassic, Jurassic, and Cretaceous Periods. *Apatosaurus* lived during the late Jurassic Period. This was about 150 million years ago.

Young *Apatosaurus* grew to full size in about ten years.

Dinosaurs went **extinct** at the end of the Mesozoic, about 66 million years ago.

Today, scientists study dinosaur **fossils** to learn about how they lived and what they ate. They compare dinosaurs with living animals. Dinosaurs varied greatly in size and appearance. Dinosaur **species** had different diets. They lived in a wide range of **habitats**.

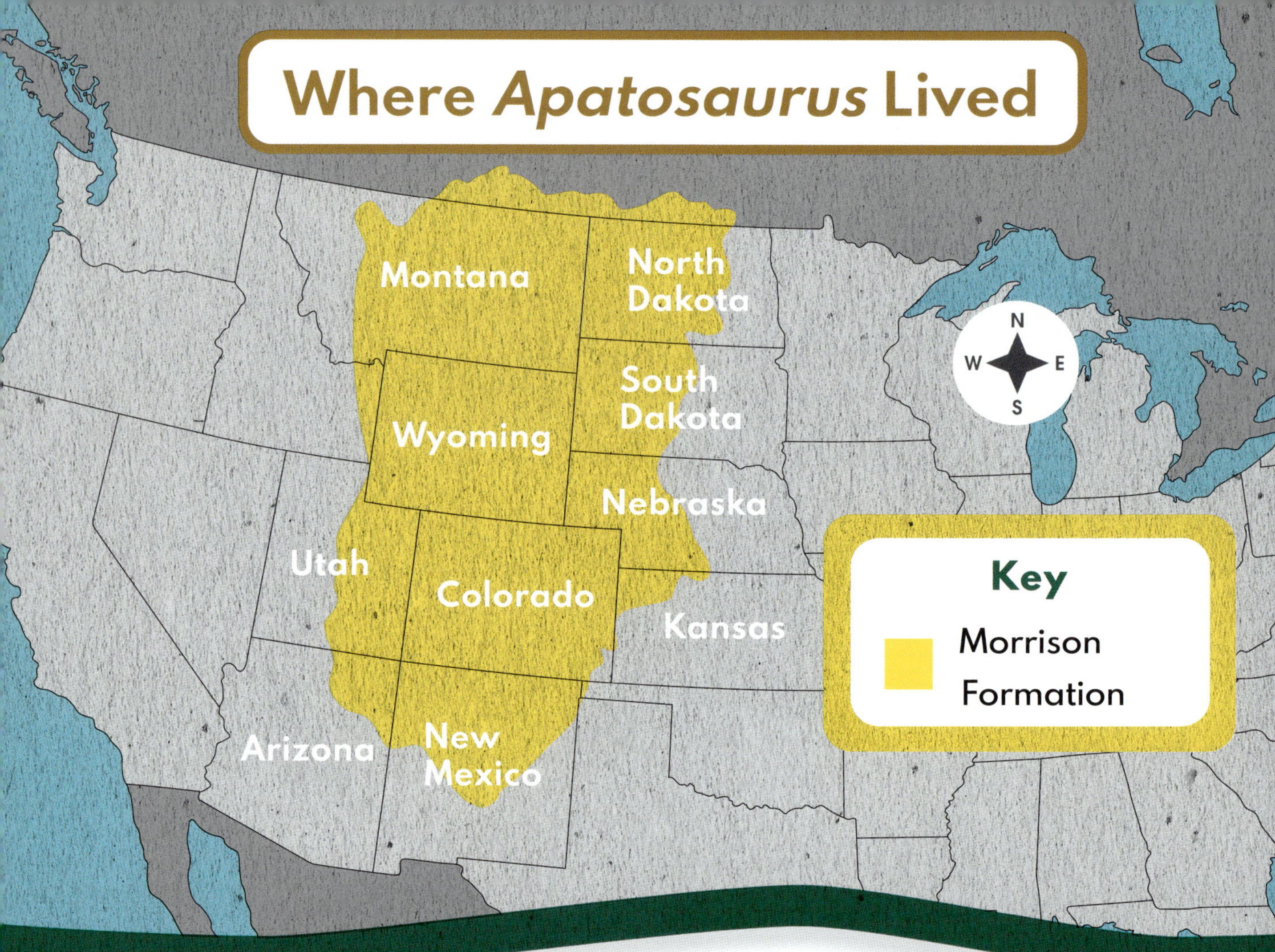

Landmasses looked very different when *Apatosaurus* was alive. Many fossils of the dinosaur were found in the Morrison Formation. Today, that is part of North America.

Apatosaurus is a type of dinosaur called a sauropod. Sauropods were plant-eating dinosaurs with long necks. *Apatosaurus* lived around 150 million years ago.

Scientists have discovered many *Apatosaurus* fossils in an area known as the Morrison Formation. This is in what is now the western United States. The Morrison Formation is a large slab of rock from the Mesozoic Era. Millions of years ago, the formation was covered by forest. It was the ideal habitat for *Apatosaurus* to thrive.

Further Evidence

Look at the website below. Does it give any new evidence to support Chapter One?

Curious Kids: Why Did the Dinosaurs Die?

abdocorelibrary.com/apatosaurus

The massive size of *Apatosaurus* kept predators away. It was one of the largest dinosaurs to ever walk Earth.

APATOSAURUS APPEARANCE

Fossils are the remains of animals and plants that lived long ago. The remains fill with soil and harden into rock. Hard body parts, including bones, can become fossils. Fossils help **paleontologists** know what *Apatosaurus* looked like.

Apatosaurus skeletons show that these dinosaurs had long necks. They also had long, powerful tails. They stood on four strong, thick legs.

Apatosaurus was a large dinosaur. It was about 69 feet (21 m) tall. This is about the length of two school buses. These dinosaurs were the heaviest known animals to roam the Morrison Formation. They weighed more than 30 tons (27 metric tons). This is about the same weight as six African elephants.

Bones are not the only parts of dinosaurs that can become fossils. Teeth and claws can turn into fossils as well. *Apatosaurus* had one claw on each front foot. It had three claws on each back foot.

A fossil of an *Apatosaurus* claw can be viewed at a museum in Tucumcari, New Mexico.

Footprints can fill with dirt and soil. These materials can turn into stone over time. They become the shape of the footprint. Paleontologists have discovered *Apatosaurus* footprint fossils. These fossils show that *Apatosaurus* had bumpy foot pads. This is similar to the feet of modern elephants. The foot pads helped reduce pressure on the feet.

Dinosaur tracks mark the ground at the Morrison Formation in Colorado.

Diet and Defense

Scientists once wondered whether *Apatosaurus* were **aquatic** creatures. Water would help support the weight of these dinosaurs. Now scientists believe that all sauropods lived on land. *Apatosaurus* had sturdy bones. They were strong enough to support its body weight.

Looking at a dinosaur's teeth can help paleontologists understand what the creature ate. *Apatosaurus* had teeth shaped like chisels.

Stone Eater

Apatosaurus swallowed stones. These did not provide energy to the dinosaur. But stones helped *Apatosaurus* digest tough plant material. They would help grind up food in the stomach.

At first, scientists thought the bones of *Apatosaurus* were similar to a sea animal.

These teeth helped *Apatosaurus* rake leaves and other plant parts into their mouths.

Apatosaurus had a long neck. Scientists think the neck was not very flexible. As a result, this dinosaur ate mostly low-lying plants.

Apatosaurus did not hunt other animals. But they were not defenseless. These dinosaurs had long, thin tails. They could swing their tails like a whip. This movement created a loud crack. The tail itself was not powerful enough to harm predators. But the noise scared predators away.

Explore Online

Visit the website below. Does it give new information about *Apatosaurus* that wasn't in Chapter Two?

Apatosaurus

abdocorelibrary.com/apatosaurus

This *Apatosaurus* skeleton is the largest dinosaur on display at Chicago's Field Museum.

CHAPTER 3

APATOSAURUS DISCOVERIES

In 1877, Arthur Lakes and Henry C. Beckwith discovered the first *Apatosaurus* fossils. They found the fossils in the Morrison Formation. The two men sent their findings to a paleontologist named Othniel Charles Marsh.

Earl Douglass, *front*, unearthed *Apatosaurus* tailbones in Carnegie Quarry in Dinosaur National Monument.

He was a professor at Yale University. Marsh named the new dinosaur *Apatosaurus*.

Earl Douglass made another major *Apatosaurus* discovery in 1909. His job was to find dinosaur fossils. His findings would be displayed at the Carnegie Museum in Pittsburgh, Pennsylvania. Douglass searched in northeastern Utah. There, he discovered eight *Apatosaurus* tailbones.

Many more bones were discovered in the area. They called the dig site Carnegie Quarry. Eventually, more than 350 tons (318 metric tons) of fossils were discovered at this site.

Paleontologists found an *Apatosaurus* skeleton at the quarry. It was missing a skull, but they displayed it anyway. The headless skeleton was at the Carnegie Museum in 1915. In 1979, an *Apatosaurus* skull was added to the skeleton. The skeleton is still on display today.

A Rare Find

Paleontologists rarely find dinosaur skulls. Skulls are hollow. They have room for the brain, eyes, and tongue. They are fragile. Skulls tend to break apart rather than becoming fossils.

People can also view *Apatosaurus* skeletons at many other museums, including the University of Wyoming.

The *Brontosaurus* Debate

Marsh also named another sauropod. This one was *Brontosaurus*. A paleontologist named Elmer Riggs took a closer look at *Brontosaurus* fossils. He did not think that *Brontosaurus* and *Apatosaurus* were different animals. In 1903, all *Brontosaurus* fossils were reclassified as *Apatosaurus* fossils.

But things changed in 2015. A study showed that *Apatosaurus* was larger than *Brontosaurus*. Scientists argued that the two should be

Apatosaurus means "deceptive lizard" in Greek.

considered different dinosaurs again. The debate is still ongoing.

In Media

Apatosaurus appears in pop culture today. *The Land Before Time* is a series of movies. It also became a TV series in 2007. One of the main characters is Littlefoot. He is an *Apatosaurus.*

Littlefoot is the *Apatosaurus* in *The Land Before Time.*

The Pixar movie *The Good Dinosaur* features an *Apatosaurus* named Arlo.

Littlefoot has orangish-brown skin. Arlo's skin is a warm green. It is hard for scientists to know the color of dinosaurs. Usually, color is not preserved in fossils. But *Apatosaurus* fossils do help scientists learn how the dinosaurs looked, what they ate, and how they behaved. Dinosaur fossils continue to fascinate people. They show the history of life on Earth.

PRIMARY SOURCE

Studies support the argument that *Apatosaurus* and *Brontosaurus* are different dinosaurs. Emanuel Tschopp is a paleontologist. He described the findings:

> Generally, *Brontosaurus* can be distinguished from *Apatosaurus* most easily by its neck, which is higher and less wide.

Source: Charles Choi. "The *Brontosaurus* Is Back." *Scientific American*, 7 Apr. 2015, scientificamerican.com. Accessed 26 Aug. 2024.

Comparing Texts

Review this quote. Does it support the information in this chapter? Or does it provide a different viewpoint? Explain how in a few sentences.

DINO DETAILS

Whiplike tail to startle predators

Four sturdy legs to support its weight

Long neck to reach distant plants
Chisel-like teeth to rake up plant material

Glossary

aquatic
lives in water

extinct
no longer exists

fossil
the very old remains of animals or plants

habitat
a place where animals or plants naturally occur

paleontologist
a scientist who studies fossils

predator
an animal that hunts other animals

species
a group of similar living things that can produce young with one another

Online Resources

To learn more about *Apatosaurus* and late-Jurassic dinosaurs, visit our free resource websites below.

Visit **abdocorelibrary.com** or scan this QR code for free Common Core resources for teachers and students, including vetted activities, multimedia, and booklinks, for deeper subject comprehension.

Visit **abdobooklinks.com** or scan this QR code for free additional online weblinks for further learning. These links are routinely monitored and updated to provide the most current information available.

Learn More

Extraordinary Dinosaurs and Other Prehistoric Life: Visual Encyclopedia. DK, 2022.

Giedd, Steph. *Stegosaurus*. Abdo, 2024.

Hulick, Kathryn. *Dinosaurs*. Abdo, 2023.

Index

About the Author

Angela Lim is an MFA student in poetry at Indiana University. *Stegosaurus* is her favorite dinosaur.